# Pip

**and the**

# Edge of Heaven

Text © 2002 Elizabeth Liddle
Illustrations © 2002 Lara Jones

Original edition published under the title
Pip and the Edge of Heaven
By Lion Publishing plc, Oxford, England
© 2002 Lion Publishing
All rights reserved

This edition published 2003
under license from Lion Publishing by
Eerdmans Books for Young Readers
An imprint of Wm. B. Eerdmans Publishing Company
255 Jefferson Ave., S.E., Grand Rapids, Michigan 49503
P.O. Box 163, Cambridge CB3 9PU U.K.

Printed in U.S.A.

08 07 06 05 04 03  7 6 5 4 3 2 1

Library of Congress Cataloging-in-Publication Data
Liddle, Elizabeth.
Pip and the edge of heaven / written by Elizabeth Liddle ; illustrated
by Lara Jones.
p.cm.
Summary: Before bed each night Pip asks his mother about God
and heaven, but he provides his own answers before his mother has a
chance to speak.
ISBN 0-8028-5257-2 (alk. paper)
[1. God—Fiction. 2. Heaven—Fiction. 3. Mothers—Fiction. 4.
Questions and answers—Fiction.] I. Jones, Lara, ill. II. Title.
PZ7.L6155 Pi 2003
[E]—dc21
2002015317

To Patrick,
in memory of Manan

# Pip
## and the
# Edge of Heaven

Written by
**Elizabeth Liddle**

Illustrated by
**Lara Jones**

Eerdmans Books for Young Readers

*Grand Rapids, Michigan • Cambridge, U.K.*

Pip liked to ask questions.
Especially at bedtime.

Sometimes, he listened to the answers.

Mostly, he liked to answer the questions himself.

When Pip was a very little boy, he asked his mother, "Mother, where is God?"

"Where do you think, Pip?"

"In heaven," said Pip. "But, Mother, where is heaven?"

Before she could answer, "I think," said Pip, "it's up."

"Why do you think it's up?"
said his mother.

"Because down is just earth,"
said Pip. "But up is sky, and I
think God is in the sky. From
the sky, God can look down on
us and look after us."

"Goodnight, Pip," said his
mother. "God bless you."

Pip grew a little, and as he grew, he learned. He learned that the earth was round, like a ball. He learned that the sky was made of air and clouds, and that air and clouds swirled all round the ball of the earth, covering it like a fleece. And he learned that beyond the sky was the moon, and the sun, and planets . . . and space.

Pip asked his mother, "How
big is heaven?

But, before she could answer, "I think," said Pip, "that heaven must be as big as space. Space is far bigger than the sky."

"Goodnight, Pip. God bless," said his mother.

But Pip wasn't happy.
"Mother, how near is heaven?
I hope it isn't very far away,
because when I die, I don't want
to go far away in space. I want
to be near you."

But, before she could answer, "I think," Pip said, "that heaven must begin here and stretch far out into space. But the edge must touch the earth."

"God bless you, Pip," said his
mother. "Goodnight."

Pip grew a little more and learned a little more. He learned that some things are hard, like houses and heads.

He learned that some things
are soft, like sofas and snow.

He learned that some things
flow, like water. And some
things are invisible, like wind.

Pip asked his mother, "Mother, is heaven invisible?"

But, before she could answer, Pip said, "I think that maybe heaven is hidden behind the things that we can see. Maybe, sometimes, when we look very carefully at things, we can just see heaven shining through.

"And maybe, when we die, we will see right through everything, and heaven won't be hidden at all."

"Maybe you're right, Pip,"
said his mother. "God bless you.
Goodnight."

Pip grew a little more and learned a little more, and he learned that there are many things you can see through—glass, ice, water, diamonds. Through the surface of a summer pond, he could dimly see another world, with strange plants and outlandish creatures.

On winter nights, through the glass of lighted windows, he could glimpse other families, with other things, living other lives.

Pip asked his mother, "Mother, is heaven strange? I don't want to go to a strange place when I die. I want to be with people I love, and creatures I know, and things I like. I don't want to go to a strange place."

"Maybe it isn't strange," said
his mother. "Maybe you'll find
all the people and things you
know and love there."

"Oh," said Pip, "then heaven must be where we begin. Maybe, here, we are really camping, but heaven will be home."

"Goodnight, Pip. Happy camping."

Pip grew a little more and learned a little more. Some of the things he learned made him sad. He learned that even people he loved could die. And that when they die, their bodies gradually become part of the earth again. That was good.

But he still missed them.

"So where do the people go, Mother?" asked Pip. "I know what happens to their old bodies when they don't need them any more, but where do they go?"

But, before his mother could answer, "I know!" said Pip. "They go where the people they love are. And where the people who love them are."

"The edge of heaven is
wherever the love is!"

"Yes," said his mother.

"Heaven," said Pip, "must be
a very funny shape."

"Pip," said his mother, "God
bless. Goodnight."

Pip grew a little more and learned a little more. He learned that when he thought about the people he loved, God was there in his thoughts too.

Pip asked his mother, "Mother, does God live at the edge of heaven?"

But, before she could answer, "I know," said Pip, "God must be where people love God."

"Yes," said his mother, "now go to sleep."

"And . . . ," said Pip, "God must be where there are people God loves. And . . . ," said Pip, "God loves everyone, so God must be everywhere."

"Yes," said his mother.

"And . . . ," said Pip.

"Pip . . . ," said his mother.

"That means," said Pip, "that everywhere must touch the edge of heaven."

"Pip," said his mother.

"And . . . ," said Pip, "I love you, Mother."

"And I love you, Pip."

"So the edge of heaven must run right through here, through us," said Pip.

"Pip," said his mother, "God bless you."

GAYLORD RG